Original title:
The Seed of Silence

Copyright © 2025 Creative Arts Management OÜ
All rights reserved.

Author: Theodore Sinclair
ISBN HARDBACK: 978-1-80566-698-1
ISBN PAPERBACK: 978-1-80566-983-8

Silence Cradles the Unheard

In a room with no sound, I sit and I wait,
A raccoon in pajamas arrives with a plate.
He whispers his dreams to the soft, cozy air,
While I chuckle aloud; does he think I'm not there?

The cat gives a glance, with a curious stare,
She ponders which secrets the shadows might share.
But silence is gold, or perhaps just a joke,
As we laugh at the quiet, the giggles provoke.

Still Waters of Reflection

A pond so serene, not a ripple in sight,
Where frogs in tuxedos discuss their delight.
They leap in the stillness, somersault bravado,
Creating a splash like a jovial opera solo!

I ponder my worries, a splash of my own,
But the frogs just roll on, like they're in the zone.
As I sigh in my mind, 'Oh, the depths of my thought,'
They croak, 'Life's a jest; it's all for naught!'

The Nest of Unvoiced Thoughts

In a tree full of laughing, bright ideas reside,
A squirrel in a sweater starts flipping with pride.
He gathers the whispers, those giggles unbound,
With acorns of nonsense, a treasure he's found.

Each twig is an echo, a chuckle that's heard,
As the winds swirl around, like a giggling bird.
He builds quite a fortress, of thoughts left unsaid,
With a sign on the door, 'Keep your silence,' he said.

Shadows of Lingering Whispers

In shadows we dance, under moonlight's soft guffaw,
As shadows exchange tales, breaking silence's law.
The mice wear their glasses, in a huddle they scheme,
Plotting out stories in a not-so-quiet dream.

Ghosts whisper secrets that tickle your ear,
While beetles play poker, a card game we cheer.
With laughter and whispers, the night passes quick,
As silence stands puzzled, feeling quite thick!

Veils of Quietude

In a garden where whispers play,
Where giggles sprout and dance all day,
A tiny voice might just be heard,
Saying, 'Shh! I'm not quite a bird!'

Beneath the soil, a joke is told,
By roots so wise, not stiff and old,
They chuckle softly, losing ground,
As tiny seeds make silly sound.

Around the flowers, secrets pass,
A daisy winks at a patch of grass,
'What's quiet like a whisper's riddle?'
'Something that just can't help but giggle!'

In this hush that makes us grin,
Where laughter hides, and we all win,
The stillness sings a playful tune,
Underneath the watching moon.

The Stillness Before The Bloom

Before the colors burst with pride,
The air is thick with jokes inside,
Petals waiting, holding breath,
'Til someone cracks, 'Is this the end?'

In the dark, a rendezvous,
Of prankish buds with nothing to lose,
They trade their quirks, they start to scheme,
'Let's spring up wild, and cause a dream!'

Hiccups of laughter start to grow,
As roots might tickle, just for show,
A daffodil ducks with a sly grin,
'Shall we begin? Let's let the fun spin!'

As moments stretch into silly pranks,
The quiet fades, as laughter ranks,
And just before the bloom's big show,
The silence winks, 'Here we go!'

Serenades of the Unseen

Whispers dance upon the breeze,
Mice in top hats sing with ease.
Invisible tunes, oh what a laugh,
Scratching notes on a gentle calf.

Cats play chess while sleeping dogs snore,
A harmonica blooms, and squirrels adore.
Invisible music fills the air,
Wiggling tunes without a care.

Nuances in Hushed Tone

Silent tickles of a feather light,
Frogs in tuxedos hop to delight.
Muffled giggles in the midnight mist,
Hush-hush, the jokes that can't be missed.

Invisible pranks on a squeaky floor,
Echoes of laughter, they all implore.
Words unspoken, they tickle the soul,
Subtle jesters keep the mood whole.

The Art of Lingering Silence

An awkward cough becomes a tune,
In the quiet, a cheeky raccoon.
Laughter lingers, tickling the ears,
While crickets curse their missing peers.

A mime walks by with a grand bouquet,
Goldfish giggle in their own way.
Songs of silence, a comical twist,
Unseen jests in a world we've missed.

Phantoms of the Mind's Quiet

Ghostly whispers in a silly hat,
Dancing shadows, where's that spat?
Hushed snickers echo through the haze,
While lost socks plot their escape ways.

Chickens in tuxedos roll their eyes,
As party balloons hide in disguise.
Silent antics in the glow of the night,
Funny phantoms take humorous flight.

Beneath the Quiet Canopy

Under leaves where whispers play,
Squirrels gossip without delay.
Beneath the branches, secrets loom,
A frog is croaking like a boom.

Trees are nodding, what a sight!
While bugs have debates, oh what a flight.
Mice conduct orchestras, mouse-sized,
In this forest, fun's unadvised.

Hushed Currents of Time

Time flows softly, like a breeze,
Ticking clocks forget to tease.
A turtle's race is quite a joke,
As shadows dance behind the oak.

Fish silently giggle, tails a-swish,
While crickets chirp to grant a wish.
The moon is winking, stars are bright,
Oh what fun, the world's alight!

The Language of Stillness

In silence, laughter blooms anew,
With giggling daisies, colors too.
A rocking chair sings soft and low,
As lullabies perform a show.

The wind tells tales of mischief small,
While shadows play a game of ball.
A cat yawns out a sleepy word,
What secrets lie in whispers heard?

In the Garden of Unheard Thoughts

Unseen flowers bloom with flair,
As rabbits dance without a care.
Thoughts skip lightly on the breeze,
While bees hold meetings 'neath the trees.

The sun hides giggles in its rays,
As flowers vie for their best ways.
A maze of secrets, fun, and cheer,
In this garden, laughter's here!

The Reserve of Reverie

In the quiet corner lies a thought,
A giggling whisper, laughter caught.
Silent plans for a jolly day,
Where chuckles bloom and worries stay.

A garden of dreams all tucked away,
Where nonsense grows and games can sway.
The dandelions, they dance around,
In this hidden plot, joy is found.

Missed chances sprout like daisies here,
Each giggle a seed, no need for fear.
With every grin, we plant anew,
In the garden of fun, where smiles brew.

Unspoken Foundations

Beneath the chatter, a grin does hide,
A ticklish secret, oh what a ride.
Words like confetti, slip through the cracks,
For laughter's the language, no need for acts.

With muddy boots, we skip through the rain,
Planting mischief, ignoring the plain.
Each silent chuckle builds a strong base,
For revelry thrives in this quiet space.

Brick by brick, we stack all the jokes,
A fortress of fun, where each laugh provokes.
In the foundations, humor takes root,
On the silence, we play, an absolute hoot!

Dormant Languages of Peace

In the folds of quiet, giggles sleep,
Whispers weave dreams that quietly leap.
A quirky wordplay, waiting its turn,
Under the surface, laughter does burn.

So close your eyes, let the silliness roll,
Nonsense waking, in every soul.
In the stillness, a chuckle is sown,
Until it's a riot, like seeds overgrown.

Each hush holds a punchline, a chuckle so grand,
An unspoken language, we all understand.
In the garden of giggles, we plant our feet,
Where peace is stitched with laughter's sweet beat.

Sowing Still Moments

In the slow of the dawn, chuckles awake,
Sowing the joy, for a laugh's gentle sake.
Each moment a patch, where silliness thrives,
In the stillness, the funniest vibes.

Step lightly through puddles of giggling grace,
Where quiet meets laughter in a warm embrace.
A funny face in the dew-kissed morn,
Giggles sprouting where dreams are born.

With shovels made of whimsy, we dig, we play,
Cultivating jests in the light of day.
Let the silence burst with funny blooms,
As we sow joy in our leafy rooms!

In the Embrace of Mute Moments

Whispers play hide and seek,
As time rolls, cheery and meek.
Birds chuckle, cats conspire,
While the clocks do nothing but tire.

Laughter drips from crooked trees,
Squirrels giggle in the breeze.
A snail speeds by in slow delight,
Painted in shadows, out of sight.

Chickens debate in feathered gossip,
While mushrooms plot, a quiet Midas.
The world chuckles in hushed tones,
As silence reigns upon its thrones.

Between the notes of a humming tune,
Lies a jest, a plump balloon.
In the corners, joy takes a stance,
Where joy and quiet love to dance.

Unraveled Threads of Tranquility

A spider spins with garbled giggles,
As daylight dims, the twilight wiggles.
Laces of silence tie up the fun,
While shadows play tag under the sun.

In a nook where few would dare,
A rabbit plots without a care.
With a thump and a hop, it starts to roll,
The quiet crew controls the soul.

Potted plants hold deep conspiracies,
As rocks chuckle at the soft pleas.
In a garden where whispers bloom,
Even the gnomes find room to zoom.

A loaf of bread dreams of a buzz,
Bouncing around with a silent fuzz.
In the warmth of a laughter so grand,
The world hums on, hand in hand.

The Labyrinth of Silent Echoes

In quiet alleys, the echoes hide,
With chuckles tucked away inside.
Each shadow dances a jolly jig,
While the streetlights flicker, all so big.

Hats sway in gentle confusion,
As whispers bear a strange illusion.
The grass is tickled by secrets soft,
Where laughter drifts and spirits loft.

A chair grins wide, its creaks tease,
While candles melt in a hush with ease.
Laughter bounces off muted walls,
As the moon sneaks in during the calls.

In corners where silence seems a feast,\nTickled minds gather like a beast.
With giggles wrapped in layers of calm,
The labyrinth sings its peaceful psalm.

Voices in the Gaps

Between the silence, whispers rest,
A symphony played at its best.
Each pause a giggle, each gap a joke,
While calendars chuckle and clocks provoke.

The crickets chat without a sound,
In hidden corners, joy is found.
Books with dust bunnies draft their dreams,
While shadows giggle and laughter beams.

The wind carries secrets, oh so sly,
A tickling touch as it breezes by.
While daisies laugh, bold and spry,
Thoughts wander under a sleepy sky.

With the whispers dancing all around,
In the gaps, the merriest sounds.
In this world where stillness thrives,
Every silence joyfully arrives.

Gardens of Reticence

In a patch of whispers, plants do grow,
With giggling daisies dancing to and fro.
The carrots chuckle, the beans hold their breath,
While broccoli plots its next veggie chess.

In corners where no one dares to tread,
A sunflower winks, 'Shh, don't wake the bed!'
The compost bin tells tales of old grime,
Three worms in a row chant a silent rhyme.

Peas in their pods play hide and seek,
While plants exchange secrets with each little squeak.
The garden holds laughter, wrapped in a hush,
Where shadows of giggles in stillness all blush.

So tiptoe softly through leaf and vine,
Join in the silence, a laughter divine.
In quiet reflections, find joy that's discreet,
Where every hush hums a soft, silly beat.

The Art of Quiet Reflection

A pot of mint murmurs, 'Let's brew a surprise,'
While herbs hold their breath, practicing lies.
The basil is hiding; the thyme marks the time,
In the garden of whispers, all things are prime.

Napping on petals, a gnome dreams away,
Chortling with crickets who dare not to play.
In stillness, they ponder the world outside,
Inventing new games where no one can hide.

Fluttering leaves share a deep, silent chuckle,
While shadows of daisies wear hats made of muckle.
The fence holds its tongue, but the gate can't resist,
A joke with no punchline hides in the mist.

The art of reflection can really be sweet,
With giggles that dance on the muted heart's beat.
In the quietest moments, joy finds its place,
Framed in the laughter of nature's embrace.

The Song Beyond Sound

In a world where noises have gone on a break,
Flowers hum tunes to the clouds as they wake.
A cricket's solo, under spotlight of stars,
Brought laughter and chuckles from nearby Mars.

The song of the silence, a symphony bright,
Where whispers conduct a marvelous night.
With daisies in chorus and whispers of dew,
The petals join in for a giggle or two.

The wind's gentle breath tickles leaves with delight,
While stillness rejoices, no need for a fight.
Fragrant tones swirl with the scent of a joke,
Where trees hold their laughter in comfortable cloak.

So dance with the stillness and sway with the breeze,
Let laughter erupt from the shade of the trees.
In moments unspoken, the joy comes around,
A secret composed in the song beyond sound.

Cultivating the Invisible

In plots rich with nothing, the magic unfolds,
Where laughter is planted, and silliness molds.
Invisible seeds in the soil of the mind,
Sprout thoughts so absurd, no peeking you'll find.

Sowing the shadows with giggles and dreams,
The air is thick laden with humorous schemes.
In the garden of quiet, where stillness is bold,
Lies treasure in silence, more precious than gold.

Petunias are gossiping, but only in hues,
With colors that laugh and blend in the muse.
Invisible roots spread beyond sight and sound,
Where humor's a flower that grows all around.

So take out your shovel and dig with a grin,
Cultivate delights with the joys that we win.
In corners unexpected, let laughter be spun,
For cultivating silence is double the fun!

The Solace of Stillness

In a world full of chatter, I sit in my chair,
Contemplating the dust bunnies all in my hair.
They swirl and they dance, carefree as can be,
Making me ponder, what's the meaning of me?

As I sip on my tea, things begin to slow,
The spoon drops with a clank, oh no, where did it go?
A moment of silence, then laughter ensues,
Was it a spoon or I, who mislaid my muse?

The cat on the shelf, claims her throne with such grace,
While plotting to steal from my cozy embrace.
I tiptoe around with an air of delight,
Wishing she'd join me in this stillness tonight.

A ghost of a giggle hovers over the room,
As shadows unite and begin to consume.
In this quiet ballet, we all find our part,
In the comedy reigning within every heart.

Journeys Through the Void

On a trip to the fridge, I venture so far,
Searching for snacks like a lost shooting star.
The echoes of munching float into the air,
Filled with my snacks, no need for despair.

I navigate corners that seem to conspire,
Why do these cheese sticks twinkle with desire?
Each bag I open whispers, 'Dig in, don't fight!'
In this void of delight, I marvel at night.

Late-night explorations ignite silly glee,
What's that under the couch? Oh look, it's just me!
In journeys of silence 'neath moon's silver glow,
I dance with the shadows, putting on a show.

What is it I'm missing? Perhaps more potato,
The secrets of cupboards, says, "Don't be a slowpiano!"
I giggle in voids where echoes collide,
On journeys of laughter, I take all in stride.

A Symphony of Unsaid Words

Staring at the wall, in a state of deep thought,
Is that a whisper, or is it just caught?
A symphony playing in the air all around,
With notes of a crumb that has just hit the ground.

The dog barks a solo, it's quite out of tune,
Yet here comes the cat, conducting with a swoon.
Each wag and each paw, a prelude to bliss,
In this odd orchestra, I can't help but miss.

When silence takes over, the laughter we save,
Composes a melody that we often crave.
Unsaid words flutter like butterflies near,
As conversations tumble without any fear.

I'd join in the chorus, but where do I start?
My voice is a wobbly, lazy piece of art.
Yet in this ensemble where quiet prevails,
The giggles crescendo through whimsical tales.

The Weight of Quiet Reflections

As I ponder the weight of thoughts floating by,
One lands on my brow, and I chuckle—and why?
Is that a wise saying or mere static hum?
Perhaps just a squirrel, shivering, and dumb.

Peering through windows where stillness resides,
I catch morning sunbeams as my mind glides.
Each beam whispers softly, 'Pay attention, dear!'
Like the weight of the cookies that I hold near.

Mirror reflections reveal such a sight,
A dance with my eyebrows, a comical fright.
In moments of silence, we gently collide,
With laughter that bubbles, no need to hide.

Quiet reflections in the midst of the fun,
Remind me of antics that all have been done.
So here's to the chuckles, the jests of the mind,
In an orchestra of silence, hilarity's kind.

The Invisible Hand of Solitude

In a quiet room, a chair does squeak,
A lonely sock, the floor does seek.
The taco truck outside, they cheer,
While I ponder life without a peer.

The cat looks wise with tiny paws,
While I discuss with walls my flaws.
A punchline lost, it wanders near,
My jokes, it seems, are missing cheer.

A shiver from the fridge's hum,
Could it be laughter? Oh, what fun!
I throw a dance, the shadows play,
In silence, they laugh, then run away.

A toast to stillness in between,
Where giggles bounce, though rarely seen.
The invisible hand waves goodbye,
As I embrace a silent sigh.

In the Silence of Dusk

The sun dips low, a grand charade,
A flock of pigeons, they invade.
While crickets tune their evening song,
I wonder where all the folks went wrong.

The squirrels debate, who gets the nut?
One makes a dash, the other, 'Tut!'
In this dusk dance, shades blend and bend,
While I pretend I'm with them, friend.

A whisper of wind, a playful tease,
Makes branches sway with utmost ease.
Yet here I sit, with cup in hand,
Snickering softly at my own plan.

So raise a glass to shadows vast,
To chuckles that echo, fading fast.
In the dusk's embrace, we find our glee,
Unseen company, just laughs for me!

The Essence of Unvoiced Yearnings

In between thoughts, a giggle stirs,
Amidst the chaos, life occurs.
A potato rolls across the floor,
Inviting me to laugh some more.

Invisible dreams float overhead,
With a side of fries and fancy bread.
I crave the humor in the void,
As silence reigns, not to be destroyed.

The plants lean closer, ears all perked,
Listening keenly, their patience worked.
Could it be that green has a plan?
To grow in secret, just like man?

In whispers soft, ideas clash,
As I unwrap my thoughts with a splash.
So here's to yearning without a sound,
In laughter's essence, joy is found!

Threads of Place Between

In every nook, a tale's been spun,
With every thread, a quirky pun.
Here lies the quilt of whispered dreams,
Stitching together silent beams.

The coffee pot hums, oh so sly,
While I argue with a toaster, 'Why?'
Crumbs like confetti scatter near,
As I celebrate this quiet cheer.

Along the walls, the shadows creep,
With giggles wrapped in secrets deep.
The air is thick with jokes untold,
In these hushed moments, joy unfolds.

Threads of place entwine, so bright,
While giggles dance in the still of night.
I cherish spaces without a sound,
In laughter found, my heart is bound!

Whispers of Creation

In a garden where giggles grow,
A cactus danced, putting on a show.
The tulips chuckled, oh what a sight,
As the daisies burst into laughter at night.

The carrots sang songs, quite off-key,
While the daisies rolled on, wild and free.
A gnome with a grin, holding a cup,
Sipped tea with a snail who couldn't keep up.

The wind told tales of cheeky chives,
While grumpy onions dodged all jives.
Each whisper grew tales, oh what a mess,
Nature's comedy—a true success!

With every rustle, the secrets shared,
Created laughter, light, and care.
In nature's choir, hilarity reigns,
Where even the quiet brings merry gains.

Silent Paths Untraveled

On a path where hiccups bloom,
A squirrel sneezed, and chaos made room.
Each pebble chuckled, each twig gave a sigh,
As a turtle raced—by racing, we lie!

Beneath a shadow, a whispering breeze,
A stubborn fly danced, doing as it pleased.
The mushrooms giggled in their small hats,
While secretive frogs were planning great chats.

A hedgehog rolled in, perfectly round,
Sharing its stories, oh what a sound!
A butterfly fluttered, full of grand dreams,
As laughter echoed through nature's seams.

In quiet lands where whispers bloom,
Every giggle dispelled the gloom.
Paths unwritten, footfalls so light,
Create a giggle, a day full of delight.

Flourishing in Quiet Moments

In stillness, a tumbleweed took a spin,
While a lone snail tried to dash and win.
A sunflower winked, held a small chat,
With a bumblebee rolling like a fat cat.

A silent rain showered, tickling the grass,
The daisies sneezed, and they did it with class.
While shadows of laughter played on the earth,
In hush-filled moments, they danced for all worth.

With laughter unspoken, joy sprouts anew,
In quietest spaces, shenanigans brew.
A whispering breeze, with a chuckle so sly,
Turned thorns into roses that danced in the sky.

Roots twirled beneath, sharing secrets galore,
Each moment of stillness unlocked a new door.
In the hush of the green, giggles soared high,
As they flourished in silence, oh me, oh my!

The Heartbeat of Stillness

In stillness so subtle, a giggle took flight,
Where leaves shared secrets, hidden from sight.
A misfit breeze, whistling an odd tune,
Made branches sway, like a comical cartoon.

The owls whispered puns in the soft twilight,
While the rabbits hopped, just out of sight.
A jester in nature, a rustle, a cheer,
The world giggled quietly, full of good cheer.

Amidst the hush, there came a loud sneeze,
A porcupine nodded, feeling the breeze.
With every heartbeat, humor takes bloom,
In the laughter of stillness, who needs a boom?

When quiet reflects, it doesn't mean dull,
In the quietest moments, life is quite full.
For in laughter and whispers, together we find,
The heart of stillness, oh so kind!

The Unsaid Between Us

In a crowded room we stand,
Words are slipping from our hands.
You reach for chips, I take a swig,
Both avoiding that weird big gig.

You laugh too loud, I snort with glee,
It's a wordless dance, just you and me.
Your thoughts are bubbles, my mind's a kite,
So we giggle under the awkward light.

We share long looks, with popcorn shared,
Avoiding topics that might be dared.
Our silence hums a funny tune,
Like cats in tutus dancing to the moon.

So cheers to us, in our quiet jest,
In the loudest silence, we are blessed.
A funny way to keep it light,
Two clowns tiptoeing into the night.

In the Echo of Absence

In a world that's loud, we find our space,
Your absent nod, thumbing through grace.
We bump elbows in a witty chat,
Words float in air, like a runaway cat.

Your eyebrows raise, like sails in wind,
My jokes are silly, but you pretend.
We laugh at nothing, it's a grand charade,
In the echoes, our silence is made.

A wink exchanged, like a secret code,
Each chuckle veils what's still untold.
Yet amongst the giggles, no meaning found,
In whispered absence, hilarity crowned.

Absurdity thrives in what we don't say,
In a circus of quiet, we play all day.
With every chuckle, the humor expands,
Two jesters adrift in a world of hands.

Enigma of Calming Tides

Like waves that roll without a sound,
We ride the tide, the lost and found.
Your grin like foam, my sighs a splash,
Together we dance in a quiet clash.

The ocean's lull is a riddle we hold,
With whispers of secrets, retold and retold.
Sand between toes, we cringe and flee,
In the wave of silence, just you and me.

We dive for humor in mermaid's lore,
With fish-eyed glances, we yearn for more.
A tide of laughter, like bubbles it flows,
In the riddle of quiet, that's how it goes.

The surf's melody, a sweet serenade,
Reminds us that silence can be well-played.
A fun little puzzle, in every wink,
The calmest sea is where we think.

Seeds of Tranquility

In the garden of grins, we plant our glee,
Words are shy, like bees on tea.
With every seed, a chuckle grows,
In secret soils where laughter flows.

You pull a weed with a funny face,
I trip on roots in this twisted place.
Our silent giggles bloom like flowers,
In the laugh of nature, we find our hours.

The wind whispers soft jokes to the trees,
As leaves rustle in a playful breeze.
Every glance is a seed full of cheer,
In the quiet moments, you draw me near.

So let's cultivate this garden of jest,
Each unspoken word a gentle fest.
In the paradise of what's not believed,
Laughing with you, I feel well-received.

A Canvas of Muted Emotions

In a world where whispers play,
Colors dance, but fade away.
Giggles bloom in shades of gray,
Painting joy in shades of fray.

Muffled laughter fills the air,
Puns that float, a silent dare.
With every smile, a funny flair,
Silly thoughts are everywhere.

Between the lines, a chuckle hides,
Where seriousness takes a ride.
In stillness, humor gently glides,
And truth with laughter always abides.

A canvas bright, yet wishy-washy,
Art of jest, forever posh-y.
In muted tones, we find it posh-y,
Who said silence can't be giddy and groggy?

Reflections in the Silence of Dawn

Morning breaks, the sun's in disguise,
Birds make jokes with sleepy sighs.
Coffee spills, the mug replies,
As silence plays with witty ties.

In dawn's embrace, the world stays still,
Yet giggles bounce on a sleepy hill.
Where dreams collide, and time must chill,
And quiet moments start to thrill.

Reflections swirl like cream in tea,
Laughter echoes, can't you see?
Each silent chuckle, a bumblebee,
Buzzing past, so joyfully free.

The clock ticks soft, but here we jest,
In dawn's hush, we're truly blessed.
With every pause, the mind's a fest,
Funny thoughts, they never rest.

Whispers in the Void

In the void where echoes creep,
Laughter hovers, wide and deep.
Silent jokes that make us leap,
Tiny secrets we must keep.

A knock-knock waits for a reply,
But all it gets is a silent sigh.
Friends chuckle at the passing sky,
Thinking of puns that float on high.

The vacuum hums a silly tune,
In its echo, we laugh at noon.
A quiet world where goofs are strewn,
And every pause becomes a boon.

Whispers dance in empty halls,
Tickling ears, with soft enthralls.
In silent realms, laughter calls,
As joy in stillness gently sprawls.

Echoes of Unspoken Dreams

In dreams unvoiced, a snicker flies,
Echoes of laughter catch our eyes.
Serious faces, but oh the surprise,
As hilarity in silence lies.

A thought drifts by, a joke so sly,
In a realm where giggles lie.
Witty remarks in shadows pry,
Finding joy where thoughts can fly.

In the quiet, puns find a way,
To bounce around and softly play.
As silence serves a funny bouquet,
With blooms of giggles on display.

Unspoken dreams break down the wall,
In chuckles, we stand tall.
When laughter brightens, echoes call,
In quietude, we have it all.

The Quietus of Time's Caress

In a hall where whispers snooze,
The clocks tick-tock in quiet ruse.
Time wears socks of fuzzy wool,
While giggling thoughts begin to drool.

A snail once tried to hold a chat,
But ended up as lunch for that.
The couch potato's lazy cheer,
Said, "I'll nap, time disappears!"

Amidst the calm, a cat will prance,
With stealthy grace, a silent dance.
She thinks she's quite the ninja queen,
But trips on dust, a silly scene.

From shadows deep, a joke takes flight,
An echo laughs—who's there, not quite?
In silence' realm, the laughter grows,
As time tiptoes on silent toes.

Hushed Gardens of Contemplation

In gardens where the giggles bloom,
The flowers whisper, making room.
A gopher's tale, a secret shared,
In quiet tones, how much he cared.

Beneath a tree with bark of bliss,
Two worms punned about the abyss.
They plotted their escape this spring,
And laughed as birds began to sing.

A beetle wears a bowtie neat,
He waltzes on his tiny feet.
With every turn, he swings and sways,
And bids farewell to mundane days.

In silence deep, a chuckle's spun,
A hedgehog's suit outshines the sun.
In gardens hush, the jokes abound,
As laughter blooms beneath the ground.

Embers of Untold Stories

The campfire crackles with soft cheer,
As shadows dance, then disappear.
A tale ignites, a ghostly spark,
But all it does is light the dark.

The marshmallows, golden, fluff away,
While crickets chirp their night ballet.
A raccoon peeks from behind a tree,
To hear a tale of jubilee.

An old log rolls, with wisdom cracked,
It chuckles soft, as tales are stacked.
Each ember whispers, "Tell it right!"
But giggles steal the waning light.

In silence shared, the stories twine,
The night wears socks—old, worn, divine.
With each bright tale, the laughter stings,
And silence lifts on cheerful wings.

Silence as a Soft Embrace

In velvet dreams where quiet rides,
The thoughts parade in funny slides.
A rabbit whispers, 'What a view,'
As pigeons plot their next big coup.

The world around is hushed and sweet,
With sticks of gum beneath the seat.
A hedgehog wraps in cozy bliss,
While butterflies share a gossip kiss.

A grumpy frog croaks, "What's the fuss?"
And silence grins from all of us.
The moon rolls by with a cheeky grin,
As laughter hides beneath the skin.

In clouds of jest, the wind is sly,
With every giggle, oh my, oh my!
Embraces soft, a hug for ears,
In silence shared, we shed our fears.

Ambience of Hidden Thoughts

In corners where whispers do hide,
The laughter of thoughts, side by side.
A sock on a shelf, a bird in a hat,
Silly little secrets, imagine that!

A tickle of giggles, oh what a cheer,
Silent chuckles sneak up from the rear.
A cat wearing glasses, how could it be?
Humorous musings that dance with glee!

Unseen jesters in a mind's parade,
Jokes that are subtle, in silence they wade.
Oh, catch that shy grin peeking around,
Hiding from echoes, yet always found!

Imagined replies in the stillness float,
Silly retorts that don't stay remote.
As walls keep this laughter, oh what a scene,
A comedy club where no one's been!

Unwritten Chapters

Between the lines of a book yet to write,
Lie characters waiting for day and night.
Mysterious plots wrapped in jest,
Scribbles of silliness, barely expressed.

A pirate who dances, a ninja who sings,
These tales of hilarity, oh what joy it brings!
Looping through dreamland, so wacky and bright,
Whispers of fun, in the soft fading light.

Each page is a canvas, each laugh a delight,
Monsters with marshmallows, what a funny sight!
A hero in pajamas, a villain with pies,
Unseen adventures, oh how time flies!

These chapters unwritten hide gags and puns,
Waiting for moments when laughter just runs.
Oh, the tales we could tell if we just let them spin,
In the margins of silence, let the giggles begin!

The Weight of Unspoken Words

A balance of banter that never was said,
Heavy on humor, light as a thread.
Invisible balloons, floating with glee,
Pushing back laughter, how can it be?

They sit in the air, these quirky remarks,
Like squirrels on bicycles dodging the parks.
With every raised eyebrow, the tension does swell,
As laughs brew beneath a soft, secret spell.

Clowns in the quiet, with pies in their hands,
Waiting for moments, making their plans.
Why shout when you can let giggles just roll?
As whispers unravel, they take on a toll.

So cling to that chuckle, don't let it just fly,
Release it in bursts, let the joy occupy!
With every unspoken, a tickle will grow,
Until the floodgates open, and laughter's aglow!

Breaths Between Frequencies

In waves of silence, oh what a spree,
Tuning into chuckles, are you with me?
Radio static with giggle-filled breaks,
A symphony silent, but oh, what it makes!

The pause between jokes, a hiccup or two,
Are we hearing whispers of something askew?
A nod to the funny, a wink to the wise,
Harmonizing humor that's bound to surprise.

Frequency flickers, like stars overheard,
Crickets are chirping, how absurd!
A bounce in the rhythm, a flutter of cheer,
As laughter's frequency draws near and near.

So dance with those beats, let your giggles resound,
Embrace every silence, let happiness abound!
For in the still moments, the fun does convene,
Whispers of laughter that remain unseen!

The Unseen Pulse

In a garden where whispers play,
A cucumber giggles, trying to sway.
Beans hold secrets, all in a jest,
While carrots prepare for a leafy fest.

A cat naps under the grapevine's tune,
With dreams of cheese floating under the moon.
The radishes roll with a purpose quite light,
Wishing for pizza to sprinkle their night.

In this lush land, the veggies converse,
Trading old stories, it's quite a universe.
A turnip sings loud, but no one can hear,
And broccoli dances, with no trace of fear.

So if you should wander to where greens abound,
Listen for laughter where joy can be found.
The silence speaks volumes, if you lend an ear,
To the chuckles of life hidden far and near.

Melodies of the Mute

In a world where quiet has a cheer,
A mouse in a tux plays a tune sincere.
The ants in a line hold a grand parade,
Marching in whispers, a sight well displayed.

The sunflowers sway in their golden caps,
Sharing tall tales, a bunch of mishaps.
A butterfly joins with a fluttering grin,
While the beetles file in with a misstep or spin.

They gather for tea, in a creaky old chair,
But the teapot's empty, oh, such despair!
Yet laughter erupts like a bubbling brook,
In the garden of quiet, take a second look.

So hear their soft whispers, the chuckles, the snares,
Among fragrant petals and tender care.
Even the shy ones have giggles to share,
In melodies humming, everywhere!

Gardens of Reverence

In the patch of the tranquil, a potato winks,
With plans for a party and thoughts on drinks.
Radishes giggle in shades of bright red,
While peas roll their eyes, 'Oh, what's being said?'

The garden gnomes listen, they nod and they cheer,
As flowers recount stories of laughter and beer.
The moonflower whispers of beauty untold,
While carrots toast life, in the evening cold.

The vibe here is funny, with jesters galore,
Even the lettuce drops quips to explore.
The broccoli stands poised, with flair and with pride,
As everyone revels, it's quite a wild ride.

So come to this place where the silence reclaims,
With echoes of laughter, and cleverest games.
In the realm of the quiet, humor's entwined,
A garden of wonders, where joy is enshrined.

Untangling Quiet Threads

In the loom of the night, the stitches align,
Where shadows tickle and stars softly shine.
A whispering breeze tells comedic tales,
Of socks misaligned, and lost porcelain scales.

The owls trade gossip, all wrapped in good fun,
While crickets compose, under moonlight's run.
The fireflies giggle with glimmering glee,
As the night's soft humor twirls with a key.

A weasel in a bow tie recites his best joke,
While hedgehogs chuckle, 'That is no hoax!'
The stars laugh along, twinkling with flair,
In the quietest moments, joy dances in air.

So listen close, dear friend, under night's tranquil dome,
Where silence unravels with a whimsical poem.
Amongst all the quiet, those threads come undone,
Spinning tales of laughter, until the rise of the sun.

Whispered Secrets of the Night

In shadows where the giggles hide,
The crickets throw a raucous ride.
A whisper slips on moonbeam trails,
While sleepy heads spin silly tales.

The owls hoot jokes that fly like kites,
While stars dance on their twinkling heights.
A secret shared with wink and nod,
But who knew the night could be so odd?

Beneath the blanket of swirling breeze,
Giggling blooms flit between the trees.
Their laughter ripples, soft and sweet,
With every rustle, oh what a treat!

As silence chuckles, sly and thin,
The joyful echoes start to spin.
In quiet corners, laughter's found,
A riot hid without a sound.

Murmurs in the Absence

When absence settles like a hat,
The mice convene for a loud chat.
They squeak and squeal in muted glee,
Finding joy in their wild spree.

A shadow winks, it knows the fun,
As two lost socks engage and run.
They tumble on the kitchen floor,
A silent party knocks at the door.

In corners where the dustbunnies spin,
Soft whispers of nonsense whirl within.
The lamps stand by, bemused yet bright,
Caught up in this raucous delight.

With giggles trapped in unseen air,
Murmurs bounce without a care.
An absence that fills up the room,
Crafting smiles amidst the gloom.

Echoing Through the Chamber of the Heart

High in the echoing hall of cheer,
A tickle of laughter draws us near.
Bouncing off walls like a rubber ball,
The heart makes noise, it can't be small.

With silly rhythms the laughter plays,
As every chamber joins the praise.
A quirk, a giggle, a booming thrum,
What's that sound? It's the heart's own hum!

With whispers cartwheeling through the night,
Each echo glows with a silly light.
The beats dance wildly, all around,
In this chamber, joy is found.

Mirth rustles through the corners tight,
Creating sparkles in the night.
An orchestra of heartbeats sing,
To the rhythm of the laughter's fling.

The Tapestry Woven in Silence

In threads of quiet, stories fly,
Where whispers spin and secrets sigh.
A tapestry hung on a wall of dreams,
Woven with giggles and silly beams.

Each stitch a chuckle, each knot a grin,
Fluffy clouds where mischief's been.
In corners wild, where shadows prance,
Silence hosts its own grand dance.

With colors splashed from laughter's bow,
A fabric thick with joy we sew.
While threads intertwine, they sparkle bright,
In this quiet riot of pure delight.

So let the needle skip and weave,
A funny tale, let's not believe.
In silence, masterpieces are made,
In laughter's quilt, we joyfully wade.

Solitude's Gentle Thrum

In a corner I sit, quite alone,
A plant in a pot, a gnome on his throne.
Whispers of nothing tickle my ear,
A chorus of crickets, loud and clear.

Echoes of laughter float by like a breeze,
Invisibly tickled, I'm far from uneased.
My friends are the shadows, they dance with delight,
Creating a spectacle, hidden from sight.

Chasing my thoughts down an empty hall,
Knocking on silence, I bounce off the wall.
Alone but not lonely, I giggle and grin,
What fun it is having oneself as a twin!

Wearing pajamas, I host a grand feast,
An army of crumbs, they munch at the least.
Tea parties with teapots that giggle and sigh,
The quieter it gets, the louder I try!

Embracing the Unexpressed

In the realm of whisper, ideas collide,
Where thoughts play hide and seek, joyfully slide.
Invisible games of charades on a loom,
I laugh with the echoes that fill up the room.

Each thought is a puppy, so lively, so spry,
Barking in silence, oh my, oh my!
Value of silence, a treasure busting free,
I hug all my secrets, they giggle with glee.

Talk without talking, a riddle we weave,
In the theater of quiet, a fun trick up the sleeve.
Glee in confusion, lighthearted embrace,
In this carnival of mind, I find my own space.

Squirrels on stilts, they frolic and prance,
As I swerve through the void, they lure me to dance.
In the chain of unspoken, we're tangled and twirled,
A jubilation of silence, my very own world!

Cultivating Quietude

In stillness, I plant my mind like a seed,
It sprouted a meadow, I chuckle indeed.
With butterflies whispering soft little plays,
I stroll through the stillness in whimsical ways.

Jokes in the quiet, oh how they adore,
Tickling the petals that dance on the floor.
As laughter erupts from the farthest of nooks,
I'm the gardener of silence, in whimsical books.

Grass grows with secrets, on paths made of dreams,
An orchestra of whispers and silly moonbeams.
Chortling with daisies who sway in the light,
Who knew being silent could feel so just right?

Creating my kingdom, a realm of pure fun,
Where sentences never come out heavily spun.
In fertile ground, I frolic and play,
With laughter as my harvest at the end of the day!

Harmony in the Abyss

Deep in the chasm where echoes reside,
Giggles flicker like stars in a tide.
An abyss filled with laughter, a paradox rare,
Where mumbles are music and silence a flare.

Navigating nonsense with an upside-down frown,
I waltz with the whimsy and paint the whole town.
Lost in the jests that the shadows disclose,
A chuckle erupts where the quietness grows.

Waves of unspoken wrap round like a hug,
I'm tapping my toe to a tune that's a shrug.
In the depths of the din, I'm twirling in glee,
Finding the merriment nestled in me.

So fear not the bleakness, shake hands with the void,
Where silence is clever and laughter's employed.
In the harmony swirling, I wobble and spin,
For the depths of the quiet hold comedy within!

Quietude's Rich Tapestry

In a garden where whispers bloom,
The silence hums, like a quiet tune.
A sneak peek at thoughts, all folded tight,
Waiting for chaos, out of sight.

Bees buzz softly, with secrets to tell,
While bread crumbs fall from a laughing bell.
The breeze brings jokes from the nearby brook,
As frogs recite lines from a funny book.

Clouds float lazily, like fluffy dreams,
Tickling the air with their wobbly seams.
Where giggles dance in the wispy air,
And silence turns playful everywhere.

A tumbleweed rolls, only it knows,
The punchline of nature, how laughter flows.
With shushed conversations wrapped in glee,
In this stillness, we jest, just you and me.

Embracing Calm Waters

In still waters, the fish make a joke,
With splashes of laughter, they lightly soak.
They tickle the surface, but stay discreet,
In silenced giggles, no one would cheat.

A duck swims past with a knowing grin,
Quacking out puns, where echoes begin.
The moon winks down with a silver beam,
Peeking at ripples, life's silly scheme.

The frogs on the bank trade odd little rhymes,
Bouncing in sync with the chimes of times.
While lilypads float with a buoyant cheer,
As nature's wise jesters draw us near.

Beneath the calm lies a shimmer of fun,
Where laughter bubbles and frolics begun.
In tranquil embrace, we find our grace,
Surrendering joy in this funny space.

Denying the Clamor

In a world full of hustle, we choose to hide,
With earplugs of laughter, we take a ride.
The hustle and bustle may want a voice,
But silence sings out like a playful choice.

A squirrel chimes in, 'Why the rush, my friend?'
As acorns drop down, they start to pretend.
That each little nut is a treasure of sound,
In stillness, they jest with joy all around.

The leaves rustle softly, sharing a pun,
While shadows play tag, they're always on the run.
The bumblebees chuckle with nectar in tow,
In this quiet chaos, emotions let go.

Through giggles and whispers, we find our ground,
In denying the clamor, we've truly found.
That sometimes the silence is ripe with delight,
With humor we dance, embracing the night.

Reverberations of Tranquil Echoes

In gentle rumbles of soft, sweet sighs,
The echoes play tag with none of the lies.
A soft chuckle from a passing breeze,
Natural music that brings us to ease.

The mountains grin wide with their rugged face,
As the valleys reply with a soft warm embrace.
The rivers rush in with a cheeky wink,
Bubbling with joy, making silence think.

A rabbit hops by, in a twitchy jest,
Sharing the secrets that nature knows best.
With each little footfall, a chuckle is made,
In this quiet refuge where giggles won't fade.

These echoes we cherish, in shadows and light,
Patterns of whimsy that dance in our sight.
With laughter and calm, side by side they blend,
In reverberations where fun knows no end.

Whispers in the Stillness

In the corners, secrets hide,
Squirrels twitch their tails with pride.
Mice wear hats and dance around,
In this hush, the giggles sound.

Invisible jokes float in the air,
A breeze catches laughter, light as a hare.
Things that shouldn't, start to sway,
As shadows play peek-a-boo all day.

Puddles reflect a silly grin,
While birds chirp, 'Let the fun begin!'
Clouds drift by in a jovial chase,
Tickling trees in a gentle embrace.

In whispers, the world weaves its glee,
As quiet chuckles dance like a bee.
So hush now, don your giggling cloak,
In this stillness, let hilarity evoke.

Echoes of Unspoken Dreams

Bubbles bounce with a giggly sound,
As dust particles whirl all around.
The sofa sighs, has something to say,
About dreams that giggle and dance in play.

Beneath the bed, a sock takes flight,
Dreams of adventure in the night.
The floorboards creak a merry tune,
As whispers tell tales of the moon.

A flying fish in a soap bubble,
Swims through wishes, no hint of trouble.
Laughter rides on silent wings,
In the stillness, joy it brings.

These echoes bounce off every wall,
Tickling fancies, big and small.
With humor wrapped in quiet charms,
We dance to the beats of life's gentle calms.

The Language of Quietude

A cat with a secret softly purrs,
As invisible laughter quickly stirs.
Chairs conspire in the softest way,
Holding secrets that tease and play.

The clock gives a wink, its hands spinning fast,
Tickling the moments, making them last.
Even the dust bunnies join in on fun,
Spinning tales of races they've run.

Whispers paint pictures of candy-coated skies,
Where cupcakes bounce and marshmallows fly.
Turtles wear hats as they waddle by,
Joining the giggles, oh my, oh my!

Hear the silence, watch it dance,
In quiet shadows, take a chance.
For in this hush, laughter reigns supreme,
Crafting delight from every dream.

Beneath the Veil of Hushing

Under soothing waves of calm delight,
Hilarity lurks, ready to ignite.
Books murmur secrets, stories unknown,
As whispers of cheeky dreams are sown.

Pillows giggle, tickling your face,
While the curtains sway, a playful embrace.
Lamps blink in Morse, a comical code,
As lazy thoughts begin to explode.

Crickets hold court, sharing a laugh,
While moths do a dance on the golden path.
Time plays pranks, bending like clay,
As we chuckle at words we can't say.

In this hush, joy takes its flight,
Beneath the veil, the world feels bright.
Listen closely, you might just see,
The funny side of tranquility.

When Words Lay to Rest

In a world where chatter dies,
The squirrels start to socialize.
Whispers flutter through the breeze,
As shy birds play hide and seek with trees.

Lizards lounge in easy chairs,
While hedgehogs claim the vacant squares.
A grumpy cat drops all debate,
And mimes the moves of a first date.

The ants conspire with great glee,
Deciding how to set them free.
With popcorn popped and jokes on cue,
They laugh so hard, it feels brand new.

So here's to silence, thick and round,
Where no loud vowels can be found.
In this quiet, humor's spun,
As nature laughs, and we have fun.

Cradle of Untold Stories

The raccoons sit with earnest looks,
As owls read from their dusty books.
Squirrels share their nutty fables,
While turtles tell of table scrambles.

With shadows playing on soft grass,
The wise frogs croak, "Let's raise a glass!"
To memories that never breathe,
To tales that hang like golden wreaths.

In this cradle, giggles swell,
As creatures weave their secret spells.
With every tale, a chuckle springs,
Now the meadow sweetly flings.

So gather round for stories weird,
Of blunders, mishaps that we've steered.
In silence, humor softly plays,
As nature winks through leafy bouquets.

Unfurling in Still Air

The daisies dance without a sound,
While bunnies hop around the ground.
Invisible giggles float on by,
As even shadows dare to sigh.

A snail with dreams of speed so grand,
Plans a race with a lazy hand.
The tortoise yells, "I'm winning, see?"
And laughs so loud, it cracks the glee.

Wind chimes jingle in the dusk,
While butterflies plot without a husk.
In quiet times, the humor's clear,
A knot of laughter, as friends draw near.

So here we yield to motion slow,
In stillness, joy begins to grow.
Where silence reigns, there's fun to share,
An unfurling tapestry in air.

Muted Horizons

In a land where giggles grow,
And whispers dance with ebb and flow.
The mountains chuckle, the rivers sigh,
As wind stirs up a playful high.

Sky-blue jays attempt to sing,
While frogs join in, doing their thing.
Every croak and chirp a note,
In the air, they humorously float.

Lazy clouds drift, in jest they tease,
As grasshoppers hop with camaraderie ease.
The sun dips low, a wink so sly,
While fireflies giggle as they fly.

So here we stand at muted sights,
Finding laughter in the nights.
In whispered tones, the fun ignites,
As silence blooms in sheer delights.

Blossoms of Taciturnity

In a garden where whispers grow,
Barely spoken, they steal the show.
A hat that's silent, a foot that's mute,
Makes flowers giggle in their roots.

The daisies dance without a sound,
While tulips wear their silence crowned.
Bumblebees buzz in soft retreat,
As giggling petals find their beat.

A quiet toast to subtle glee,
Where laughter's hidden in the leaves.
Who needs a roar when hush is gold?
In stillness blooms the stories told.

So let the quiet artists thrive,
For in their calm, the jokes arrive.
While secrets bloom in specter light,
Our giggles tend to take their flight.

The Silence That Nurtures

In a field where giggles sleep,
The hush can cackle, oh so deep.
With mushroom hats in still display,
Who knew they'd steal the scene today?

The butterflies tiptoe with glee,
In a silent world, just let it be.
A squirrel snickers, sans any sound,
As whispers tumble to the ground.

Where silence feeds the seeds of fun,
And laughter hides from everyone.
A mouth that's shut, a grin so wide,
In quiet realms, our joy resides.

Let's plant a laugh without a word,
And watch it flourish, quite unheard.
For in the hush, absurdity,
Grows wildly forth, as purest glee.

Voices Beneath the Surface

A pond reflects a silent scream,
With frogs and fish, they plot and scheme.
Their jokes float softly, just beneath,
As minnows laugh with toothy wreath.

An otter waddles, quiet and sly,
While turtles roll their eyes nearby.
With giggles lost in waves that sway,
Fish find new ways to joke and play.

A quiet splash, a tickled tail,
Echoes dance but no one wails.
In sub-aquatic, laughter spins,
As bubbles rise from where it begins.

So hold your breath and dive below,
Where secret chuckles steal the show.
In muted depths, the funniest meet,
In silence, water holds their beat.

In the Calm Between Notes

In melodies where silence hums,
Between the beats, the laughter drums.
With staccato hiccups, notes collide,
While chuckles linger, shyly bide.

A maestro lifts his wand to cue,
But in the pause, the giggles brew.
The triangle chimes, the clarinet sighs,
Yet whispers layer in playful lies.

The crowd awaits the somber sound,
But in the quiet, joy is found.
While violins play sad and sweet,
A feathered joke makes all hearts leap.

So let the music softly play,
In silent laughter, we'll find our way.
Through every pause, our spirits dance,
In quiet laughter, life's whimsy prance.

Veils of Quiet Contemplation

In corners of the room they sit,
With laughter trapped, not giving a wit.
Whispers and giggles, a silent parade,
Who knew such noise could just fade away?

In each knowing glance, they craft a joke,
While others think they're just a yoke.
A chuckle stifled, a hiccup held tight,
As libraries wrestle with ticklish delight.

A pause so thick, with humor it bends,
No need for a punchline, just playful friends.
The space between words, a tickle of glee,
Who knew quiet could be so quirky?

So here's to the giggles we swallow and bite,
In the veils of silence, we find pure delight.
With each muffled laugh, new tales will arise,
From whispers that spark, like sly fireflies.

The Depths of Muffled Reverie

Deep in the quiet, a riot unfolds,
With secret handshakes, and stories retold.
Each word a gem, polished by thought,
What fun is silence? The battle is fought!

Sipping our tea, we raise our sly brows,
As thoughts tangle up in the intermissions' bows.
Our minds do the tango, while lips barely part,
The drama's all there, without any art.

Inside our heads, a carnival thrives,
With balloons of silence where laughter derives.
We snicker in shadows, our minds take a spin,
What's said in the silence, is where fun begins!

A murmur, a grin, a wink shared in jest,
In reverie's depths, we treasure the zest.
The ruckus of thought, so joyful and sly,
In silence, my friends, we let the fun fly.

The Hidden Chorus of Still Voices

A symphony played without any sound,
Where each inner chuckle bounces around.
Harmonies linger in the ponderous air,
In the stillness, we find the loudest fair.

Faces like statues, but giggles take flight,
Each thought is a note, a comical sight.
The sergeant of stillness, with baton of glee,
Conducts all the muses that yearn to be free.

From the depths of the quiet, a melody swells,
In shadows of silence, a joy that compels.
When whispers are wild, and secrets run deep,
The comedy's rich; it makes silence leap!

So hush of a moment, embrace all the cheer,
For the quietest laughter, is what we revere.
With a wink and a nod, our serious plight,
Turns into pure fun, in the stillness of night.

The Serenity of Unexpressed Thoughts

In the garden of thoughts, so silent, so still,
The peace of the ponder, with laughter to spill.
A look here, a nod there, the antics unfold,
As giggles in moments remain uncontrolled.

The wisdom of silence, a jest waiting there,
Like an egg waiting ample, to spring through the air.
We muse without words, with each hidden laugh,
In the calm of the quiet, the best part's the gaff.

Who knew a still moment would be such a tease?
The thoughts in their chambers just giggle with ease.
A chuckle in waiting, a whimsy unsaid,
In the serenity blooms, what joy lies ahead!

So let's toast to thoughts that do tiptoe and play,
Where silence is golden, but laughter's the way.
To the jesting of stillness, our hearts take a flight,
In unexpressed musings, we find pure delight.

Shadows of Unsung Melodies

In the corner, shadows dance,
With whispers lost in a silly trance.
Balloons float by, and then they pop,
A quiet giggle from the mop.

A cat with socks, what a sight,
Humming tunes in the dim moonlight.
The chairs join in, they creak with glee,
While the fridge plays tunes, oh, can't you see?

Laughter trails like dust in air,
Tickling toes without a care.
A mouse in boots steps on the stage,
Reciting tales in absurd rage.

The walls sway back, they hum along,
A symphony of the slightly wrong.
Where giggles twirl and silence sighs,
In silly notes, the world complies.

Quietude's Embrace

In the corner, a chair sits still,
Whispers of socks, oh what a thrill!
The cactus tells jokes, spiky and bright,
While curtains wave, all in delight.

Potatoes plot in the pantry's gloom,
Dreaming of trips to the kitchen's room.
They're making plans to ride the spoon,
Under the light of a friendly moon.

A snail in a hat with a feather grand,
Swags through crumbs like a rockstar band.
Who knew silence could sway so bold,
Like stories of veggies, confidently told?

And oh, the cracks in the walls, they grin,
As laughter echoes, let the fun begin!
In hushed embraces, joy rides high,
A quiet ruckus, oh my, oh my!

Threads of Serenity

In a world where buttons softly hum,
A quiet dog plays a tiny drum.
The clock on the wall prefers to snooze,
Counting sheep in its own cute muse.

A sink full of spoons has a comedy show,
Telling tales of what they do and don't know.
Teapots whistle tunes of love and cheer,
As chairs chuckle, 'Hey, we're still here!'

A rubber ducky joins the parade,
With bows and ribbons, it's quite the charade.
While silence wraps the room tight and neat,
Making moments feel joyous and sweet.

Lost in threads of the mundane jest,
Where the oddest things truly feel blessed.
Laughter blooms where whispers do roam,
A cozy chaos, a quirky home.

Where Silence Blooms

In a garden where shadows play peek-a-boo,
A snail wears a cape, yes, it's true!
The daisies giggle with petals aglow,
While quiet breezes put on a show.

A mole with glasses reads under the tree,
Debating with ants on how it should be.
'Should we dance or just loaf about?'
Says the wise little toad, full of clout.

The hedgehog spins tales, though spiky and round,
While the bees buzz tunes that drift all around.
With laughter like echoes, they share their delight,
In the hush of the garden, from morning till night.

In the stillness, the quirks take their flight,
Whispers weave laughter, an amusing sight.
In moments of quiet, where joy fully blooms,
The funniest things gather like dust in the rooms.

Fluttering in Stillness

In a garden so still, the flowers do grin,
A busy bee buzzes, trying to win.
A leaf flutters by, in a slow-motion race,
They all stop to stare, then break into space.

A snail sneaks a peek, with a shell like a throne,
In a world so serene, he's never alone.
With whispers of laughter and a tickle of breeze,
Even the shadows are swaying with ease.

A chorus of crickets joins in the fun,
As sunlight retreats, the dance has begun.
They jiggle and wiggle, in darkness they thrive,
In this hushed little realm, who knew they could jive?

So hush now, dear friends, don't break all the bliss,
In the silence, there's giggles, a whimsical kiss.
From the roots to the sky, in this jovial fold,
Nature's best jesters, their stories unfold.

Secrets of a Silent Seed

In the depths of the soil, a tiny tale brews,
A whisper of mischief in dirt-chuckling hues.
The seed dreams of laughter, of sun and of rain,
While worms tell old jokes that are never quite plain.

It stirs in the dark, wishing for light,
A budding comedian, itching for flight.
When it finally sprouts, it rebels with a cheer,
Producing green leaves that tickle the ear.

Buried beneath, it learned from the wise,
One wise old acorn went straight for the prize.
"Why hold all the silence while laughter can grow?"
It chuckles and wiggles, all ready to show.

So out from the soil, it stretches and beams,
In a world full of giggles, it dances in dreams.
The secret of silence, a spark held inside,
Is the laughter we carry, let's show it with pride.

Echoes in a Quiet Garden

In a quiet garden, where giggles still echo,
The daisies converse in a hushed little meadow.
With whispers of petals, they share all their jokes,
While bumblebees chuckle at sweet honey folks.

A statue just stands, with a grin on its face,
It guards all the gaffes of this cozy space.
The vines twist and twirl, looking for lines,
In the routine of quiet, where humor entwines.

While friends plant their thoughts in the soil of delight,
With a sprinkle of laughter, everything feels right.
The moon peeks and giggles at shadows so bright,
In the echoes of stillness, it's a comedic sight.

So linger a while in this tranquil embrace,
Where laughter and silence share a warm space.
In the garden of whispers, let chuckles be found,
In the dance of the quiet, where joy knows no bounds.

Soft Seeds of Reflection

In the still of the night, soft murmurs take flight,
As the stars sit and giggle, a radiant sight.
The moon, quite a joker, plays peek-a-boo skies,
While dreams sprout like daisies, with mischief and sighs.

Each seed that we plant holds a story so bright,
Of humor and wisdom, of laughter and light.
As whispers from shadows create mischievous tales,
The garden erupts with giggles and flails.

A breeze full of chuckles floats through the night,
As we ponder the wonders that shimmer in sight.
The soft seeds of thoughts bloom in playful delight,
Encased in the stillness, they take graceful flight.

So gather your giggles and plant them with cheer,
In this garden of quiet, where joy flourishes near.
From the roots to the branches, let laughter ensue,
In the dance of reflections, find the humor that's true.

www.ingramcontent.com/pod-product-compliance
Lightning Source LLC
Chambersburg PA
CBHW051641160426
43209CB00004B/740